Amazing Colours

Nicola Baxter

W
FRANKLIN WATTS

Schools Library and Information Service

S00000623200

KU-189-256

Colours are fun.
How many different colours
can you see in this picture?
What is your favourite colour?

Without colours everything looks
very different.

Here are three very important colours.
They are called primary colours.

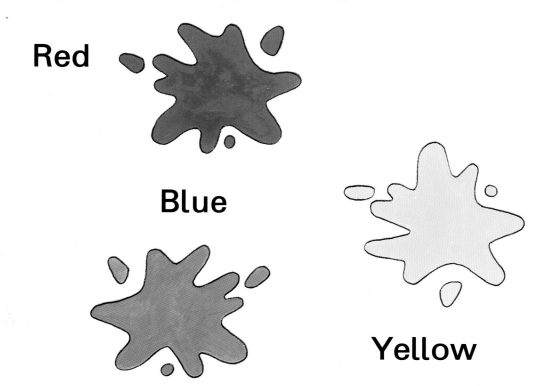

Red

Blue

Yellow

Do you know why these
colours are special?

5

The primary colours are special because they can be mixed together to make lots of other colours.

Blue mixed

 with

yellow makes... green

Red mixed

 with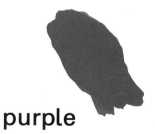

blue makes... purple

Yellow mixed

 with

red makes... orange

Try this later
What do you think happens if you mix
all three primary colours together?
Have a go yourself!

There are many blue things in the picture.

Are they all the same blue?

How can we describe the different shades of blue?

Colours can help us to sort things out...

or match things up.

Colours can help us to tell if
fruits are ripe and ready to eat...

or how something might taste.

Can you guess the flavours of these lollies?

   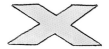 

Colours can help to make things
easy to see.

When do we need to see things clearly?

Try this later
Paint a big red cross,
a big yellow cross and
a big black cross on white paper.
Which one is easiest to see
from the other side of the room?

What happens if you use black or blue paper?

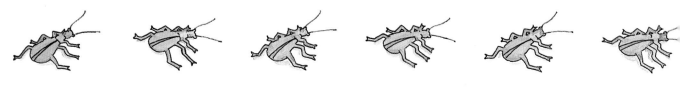

Colours can help to make things difficult to see, too.

If you were an animal, why would you like not to be seen?

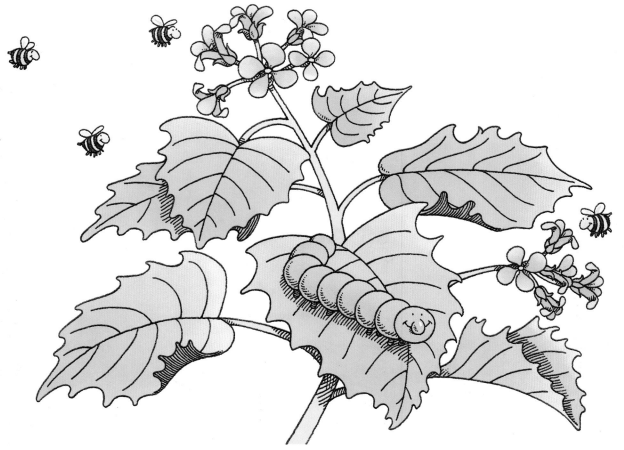

The colour of the arctic fox helps it hide from its enemies and prey.

By using paints, we can change the colour of even very big things.

Dyes are used to colour threads or fabric.
Sometimes we dye our clothes
by mistake!

The world we live in is full of changing colours.

The colour of the sky helps us to know what the weather will be like.

The colours of leaves remind us what time of year it is.

We use colours all the time.
They can help us to understand things.
They can make everything more fun.

Now try this...
Do you notice colours?
Don't look before you answer!

What colour are your eyes?
What colour is the front door of your school?
What colour shoes are you wearing?
What colours are there on the cover of this book?

Index

© 1995 Franklin Watts
This edition 2001

Franklin Watts
96 Leonard Street
London EC2A 4XD

Franklin Watts Australia
56 O'Riordan Street
Alexandria, Sydney, NSW 2015

ISBN 0 7496 4146 0

Dewey Decimal Classification
Number 535.6

A CIP catalogue record for this book is
available from the British Library.

1 2 3 4 5 6 7 8 9 10

Editor: Sarah Ridley

Designer: Nina Kingsbury

Photographer: Peter Millard

Illustrator: Michael Evans

The publishers would like to thank
Carol Olivier, Annique Simpson, Gavan
Keating, Jason Botross and Shazia

Hussain of Kenmont Primary School for
their help with this book.

Additional photographs: Bruce
Coleman 17; Eye Ubiquitous 18; Chris
Fairclough Colour Library 14; James
Davis Travel Photography 20; Robert
Harding Picture Library 12; ZEFA 2, 3.

Printed in Malaysia